G000272965

Gardening for God

by
Jane Mossendew

*Dedicated to Monsignor Guido Marini,
Master of Papal Liturgy
and Rev Prior Mark Daniel Kirby OSB,
Stamullen Co Meath.
Commemoration of St Frances of Rome,
9th March 2012.*

*All booklets are published thanks to the
generous support of the members of the
Catholic Truth Society*

CATHOLIC TRUTH SOCIETY
PUBLISHERS TO THE HOLY SEE

Contents

Warning: Do not take any herbal remedy, purchased or homemade, without the approval of a qualified medical practitioner. Sensitive skin reacts badly to some plants.

Scriptural background: from Genesis to Revelation

The first Adam fell in a garden; the Son of God, 'the second Adam', was entombed and rose from the dead in a garden. In the Garden of Gethsemane we see Jesus, the 'Son of Man', in unspeakable agony, reversing the first human sin of disobedience in giving Himself in perfect obedience to the will of the Father. In Genesis Adam and Eve were exiled from the garden in order to protect the tree of life from their grasp. After having eaten the forbidden fruit they knew good and evil, and as God says, had 'become like one of Us'. If they ate also from the tree of life, they would 'live forever' (*Gn* 3:22). God's justice could not permit disobedience to be so easily rewarded with immortality, not until that sin had been reversed and a price paid, until we came to realise the enormity of our debt. We were not to know how this would be achieved until God in and from His inestimable love and mercy sent His own Son to pay that price. Until then the tree of life would remain inaccessible to us.

The tree of life

'Now there was a garden in the place he was crucified, and in the garden there was a new tomb in which no one had ever yet been laid. And so, because it was the Jewish day of Preparation, and the tomb was nearby, they laid Jesus there' (*Jn* 19:41, 42). The Passion and death of Jesus, atoned for all human sin, including the first one. Through that atonement He unbarred the way to the tree of life, which itself features tellingly in the Book of Revelation. As part of His message to the church at Ephesus, Christ promises, 'To everyone who conquers, I will give permission to eat from the tree of life that is in the paradise of God' (*Rv* 2:7). This is explained and emphasised in the final chapter where John describes his vision of the New Jerusalem. 'Then the angel showed me the river of water of life, bright as crystal, flowing from the throne of God and of the Lamb through the middle of the street of the city. On either side of the river is the tree of life with its twelve kinds of fruit, producing its fruit each month; and the leaves of the tree are for the healing of the nations. Nothing accursed will be found there anymore' (*Rv* 22:2). 'Blessed are they who wash their robes, so that they will have the right to the tree of life and may enter the city through the gates' (*Rv* 22:14). God's edict of banishment from the tree of life is reversed. Finally, Jesus Himself issues a warning through John, that 'if anyone takes away from the words of the book of this prophecy, God will take away that person's share in the tree of life and in the holy city, which are described in this book' (*Rv* 22:19). Jesus has gained the possibility that we may inhabit the new Jerusalem, a possibility which was

totally ruled out by the original sin of disobedience. But
we may still risk losing it by disobeying His warning. Thus
concludes the Biblical record of the essentials I believe
that God wanted us to know about His Salvific plan.[1]

Symbolising the tree of life in your garden

There are several different trees, the Elder for example,
whose wood is traditionally associated with the Cross of
Christ. There is however a tree whose folk name is 'tree
of life', the **Thuya Occidentalis; Arbor-vitae**. By happy
accident, or perhaps through one of Blessed Cardinal
Newman's 'little providences' of God, before I knew any
of the lore of the tree I had already planted a thuya hedge
along the eastern boundary of my plot and also to form
the eastern and southern sides of the enclosure of what is
now my Sanctuary or Gethsemane Garden. Aside from any
spiritual significance, this evergreen is hardy to 50 feet and
can be grown as a single subject reaching a maximum of 60
feet but with regular trimming it makes a fine dense hedge
or windbreak. Remove sun or wind scorch while damage
is minimal, otherwise unsightly gaps will be left, spoiling
the protective purpose and symbolism of the hedge. Many
cultivars are available, varying in size and colour, and
therefore the tree of life is versatile in garden planning.
The bark is reddish and the foliage sometimes turns
bronze in winter. The whole plant is beautifully aromatic
when brushed or cut. Among the most popular varieties

is **Thuya occidentalis 'Rheingold'**, as its golden foliage can be relied upon to cheer the cold winter days when the garden is short of colour. The ancient Greeks used it as a purification element in sacrificial ritual, and indeed its name is from the Greek 'thujo', meaning sacrifice. In plant lore the tree symbolises stability as well as immortality, and the Catholic Church consecrated it on the Feast of the Immaculate Conception in 1862. European explorers found it in the eastern part of North America and it was one of the first to be introduced to Europe from there.

Our desire for the fruit of the tree of life

In week 2 of Eastertide, the first Office readings take us through the Saint John's encounter with the Son of Man as recorded in the Book of Revelation and we read of His messages to the seven churches. John then sees the worship of heaven as being in direct contrast to the imperfect condition of the earthly Church. Five of the seven churches show features that prevent them from attaining to the fruit of the tree of life, which is Christ Himself. At Ephesus there was a lack of love for Christ, and of others. Surely no one living in the developed world can fail to draw modern parallels with this church and with the four others who are directly addressed. At Pergamum, false teaching and pagan practices had been allowed to creep in; at Thyatira there is compromise with immorality; at Sardis there is apathy, indifference and self-satisfaction; at Laodicea lukewarmness, complacency, blindness to individual faults and an over-emphasis on civic pride.

Only at Smyrna and Philadelphia do the churches meet with Christ's approval and receive His encouragement. In them is found the character we must emulate in our desire for the fruit of the tree of life. At Smyrna the church is materially poor, but rich in spirit. Christ assures its members that their sufferings will be limited and promises them eternal life.

The Philadelphian church is outwardly unimpressive and lacking in prestige; it is an example of effective work being done for Christ, not by the strong but by the faithful.

The motif of Christ as the Tree of Life runs through this week's Office, but on Friday St Theodore the Studite (759-826) meditates on the cross itself as the tree of life. Referring to the expulsion of Adam and Eve from Paradise, he says, 'of old we were poisoned by a tree, now we have found immortality through a tree'. The reading calls to mind the anonymous early ninth century poem, The 'Dream of the Rood', praying as it does:

'…May the Lord be a friend to me,
he who suffered once for the sins of men
here on earth on the gallows-tree.
He has redeemed us; He has given life to us,
And a home in heaven.'

Indeed the presence of a Thuya hedge in your garden is a potent and living help towards prayer, and meditative study of the Scriptures. Until the prophesies at the end of the book of Revelation are fulfilled we must live in exile from the tree of life. But it is not to be an eternal exile. The Incarnation, life, death and resurrection of Jesus makes us certain of that and so we live in hope. Many writers before me have seen gardening as an expression of nostalgia for Eden and as an attempt to regain the paradise lost at the Fall. That might be true on purely psychological or folkloric levels, but it takes no account of the spiritual growth, that is made possible by the pursuit of the activity. Many people find gardens to be places of peace and refreshment. Every garden is a potential place of prayer. The present booklet attempts a brief demonstration as to how that potential can be developed and fulfilled. We have seen above how God Himself used a garden environment in salvation history, but gardens feature more than fifty times in the Old Testament, either as a setting for an actual event (e.g. Naboth's Vineyard I Kings 21), or as backdrop for mystical poetry (e.g. The Song of Solomon) Not only this, but garden related imagery is often notable, for instance in the psalms and prophets. Readers who regularly recite the Divine Office will already know how true this is; those not so familiar will find that their gardening and prayer life can be enriched by more frequent reading from the Old Testament. In fact they will increasingly see that the links between prayer and gardening are inextricable.[2]

Plants and horticultural imagery in the life
and teaching of Jesus

If God the Father was the first Gardener, it should be no surprise that His Son, as second Person of the Holy Trinity should have had such intimate knowledge and understanding of good garden practice and to have repeatedly used it in his teaching as a metaphor for spiritual planting and growth. His Parable of the Sower is the best known from the point of view of planting. Healthy growth and what the Vine Grower must and will do to ensure it, is an extended metaphor of spiritual development, and of the constitution of the Tree and its branches, that is of Christ and His body, the Church. These two texts are examples of how the very acts of sowing and pruning can lead you to meditation and prayer as you garden.

Synoptic Gospels

Of trust in God and against worry - The lilies of the field
Mt 6:25-34; *Lk* 12:22-28
The tree and its fruit – *Mt* 7:15-20; *Lk* 6:43-45
The harvest is great, the labourers few – *Mt* 9:35-38
Plucking grain on the Sabbath – *Mt* 12:1-8;
    Mk 2:23-28; *Lk* 6:1-5
A tree and its fruit – *Mt* 12:33-37
Parable of the sower – *Mt* 13:1-9; *Mk* 4:1-9; *Lk* 8:4-7
Parable of the sower explained – Mt 13:18-23;
    Mk 4:13-20; *Lk* 8:11-15

Parable of weeds among the wheat – *Mt* 13:24-30; 36-43
Parable of the mustard seed – *Mt* 13:31-33; *Mk* 4:30-32;
   Lk 13:18-19
Jesus and Zacchaeus - *Lk* 19:1-10
Parable of the wicked tenants - *Lk* 20:9-26
Labourers in the vineyard – *Mt* 20: 1-16
Jesus curses the fig tree – *Mt* 21:18-22; *Mk* 11:12-14
The landowner and the vineyard – *Mt* 21:33-44;
   Mk 12:1-12;13:28-31
Jesus denounces the Scribes and Pharisees – *Mt* 23:23-25
The lesson of the fig tree – *Mt* 24:32-35; *Mk* 11:20-25;
   Lk 21:29-22
The parable of the growing seed – *Mk* 4:26-29

Saint John's Gospel

12:24 'Unless a grain of wheat falls into the earth
   and dies…
15:1-17 'I am the true vine and my Father
   is the vine grower…'

Gardens in the history of European Christendom

Gardening is not merely a blind sentimental nostalgia for Eden, but rather a positive, energetic and rugged expression of our hope, as inspired by our faith in God, and as an application of present horticultural science. That knowledge is impressively demonstrated on a single site in England at Tim Smit's 'Eden Project' near St Austell in Cornwall.[3] However, our will to create a prayer garden, although it will be supported by scientific knowledge, springs more from our spiritual yearnings and is much closer to the impulse that resulted in our great cathedrals and abbeys. Early monastics were arguably the first, and the most influential, in uniting spiritual meaning with practical necessity and learning, as records of original monastery gardens show beyond doubt. As well as the monastic contribution, knowledge of the medicinal properties of plants was brought to Europe by pilgrims returning from the Holy Land and by soldiers homeward bound from the Crusades.

Celtic monasticism and the Desert Fathers

It could be argued that Celtic Christianity, by its mystical emphases and its sense that humanity is within nature, had an equally important effect on the development of monastic gardens in Britain. As an example, during the seventh century monks founded a monastery on the tiny Irish island of Skellig Michael about ten miles off the coast of Kerry. Theirs was a will to retreat to the 'desert' much as Saint Antony of Egypt had done some four centuries earlier, not merely as a means of escape from the world, but as an attempt to enter more deeply into the contemplation of God and to live a life of penance and self-denial. Even in this inhospitable environment the monks created small gardens for food, and possibly for the even greater solitude and protection afforded by the stone walls that surrounded them. They are a far cry from the meticulously planned Monastery gardens of the later medieval period and were small domestic havens where the monks provided food, water and shelter, not only for themselves but for other lower orders of God's creation. They appear as slightly wild, as if they want to be absorbed in God's plan, rather then to impose human organisation upon it. The Carthusians, rather than Benedictines would seem to be their natural descendants.

A modern connection – Celts and Carmelites

If your land is barren and stony, if the soil has been polluted or damaged, or if your spirituality is Carmelite or tends toward the eremitic, then perhaps a **wilderness garden** may have a practical and spiritual appeal. As we have seen, the monasticism of the Irish, Welsh and Cornish was a response to the practice of the early Desert Fathers and hermits. Whether you decide to embrace the challenge and struggle of making a desert garden, out of necessity, or from a desire to offer God your own Celtic 'green martyrdom', the result will take you back to the earliest centuries of our faith. You will become a living descendant of those monks of Skellig Michael. If you take into account the history and traditions of the Carmelite order you will in a sense be walking and working in the footsteps of the prophet Elijah.

Shrubs and trees for the 'desert'

In Victorian times the **Juniper** signified protection and asylum. This was probably because the 'Authorised Version' identifies it as Elijah's refuge during his flight from Jezebel's vengeance. His tree was probably a **broom** of the low growing straggly variety that still grows in the Holy Land. We are told that he sat down under it. I do not think it fanciful to imagine that it was the first thing he encountered that afforded any protection at all. He may have crawled under it in traumatised exhaustion and despair. The presence of either shrub will be a constant stimulus to meditation on the lessons taught by Elijah's being sustained by the angel in order that he may continue to Mount Horeb where he will hear the 'still small voice' of God (I K 19). From the ridge of Mount Carmel Elijah's servant had seen the rain cloud that ended the drought (I K 18:44). Even in a desert garden one could commemorate that event by including a water butt, and growing a **willow** and some **blackberries** in close proximity.

Flowers and herbs

'The wilderness and the dry land shall be glad, the desert shall rejoice and blossom; like the crocus it shall blossom abundantly' (*Is* 35:1).

Wild flowers can be a rewarding option, since even today many flourish in waste places on poor soil. Wild gardens have become increasingly popular and therefore a wide choice of seeds has become more readily available. In this way you will be preserving for God, those of His plants that our intensive farming methods have threatened with extinction. Of the more resilient subjects **Saint John's Wort**, will not only evoke the Baptist, that man of the Desert and 'voice crying in the wilderness', but will also provide a splash of brilliant yellow in the garden. I do not aim deliberately at a 'desert' garden, but the overall effect is of an admixture of wild and cultivated. I welcome the annual invasion of vibrant red **wild poppies**, and the clear blue of **Speedwell**, their seeds having been blown on the wind from neighbouring fields.

The Benedictine influence

Not by accident do I later describe my garden as a 'roofless outdoor sanctuary' and as that 'precious little enclosure of my heart'. The Rule of Saint Benedict was to have tremendous influence not only on monasticism but also on the development of Western culture, as masterfully described by Pope Benedict in his address to the Paris College des Bernardins in 2008, The dissemination of that Rule throughout Europe was definitely assisted in the 8th century by the English missionary Saints Willibrord and Boniface, the latter inspiring imperial decrees making it obligatory for all monasteries. Benedictine Abbeys were centres of learning in several fields other than scripture and theology. Botanists, herbalists and gardeners owe much of their knowledge to Saint Benedict's monastery at Monte Cassino. About the year 1000 ancient classical and Arabic documents were brought there for the monks to translate, copy and distribute. One of these was originally in Latin (c.400) by Apuleius Platonicus and was eventually translated into Anglo-Saxon. It did not survive but a herbarium made about 1050 combines the work of Apuleius and Dioscorides, author of the influential '*De Materia Medica*'. This herbarium is in the British Library in London and there are other late eleventh-century copies in the Bodleian Library at Oxford. All show clearly that a tremendous amount of information was being discovered and disseminated at the time. And the well-spring for all of it was Monte Cassino, and other monasteries from where foundations spread across Europe to Britain. Monks and Nuns (as witness Hildegard of Bingen, 1098-1179) were at the centre of learning about herbal treatment of all kinds of diseases and of knowledge of the cultivation and harvesting of plants. Information about growing crops and keeping livestock, particularly sheep, was exchanged. And so it is impossible to overestimate the contribution of Benedictines and Cistercians to our present horticultural and agricultural knowledge. For this reason, I dedicate all my gardening to Our Lady Seat of Wisdom and to Saint Benedict and his sons and daughters down the ages.

The medieval monastic garden

The Swiss Monastery of St. Gall, founded 613, has become a template of the classic medieval monastic garden layout. Very little of the original monastic complex remains (The present-day Cathedral was not built until the middle of the 18th century). Surviving plans are the clearest available indication of its organisation. Study will reveal how you can incorporate, or at least suggest, some of the commonly found features of monastic gardens into your own, however small and humble it may be (Google 'Abbey of St Gall Images' to select plan).

Orientation of the Abbey and its Church

'My sister, my spouse, is a garden enclosed…' (*Sg* 4:12a). The Abbey Church and its altar faced towards the East, that is towards Christ as the 'Morning Star' and in the direction of His Resurrection and longed-for Second Coming. It was there that the monks or nuns recited or sang the Divine Office, which apart from the celebration of Holy Mass was the chief purpose of their lives. Even if your garden is not focused 'ad orientem' you should be able to have an eastward facing stone or cross to represent not only the Abbey church but the Universal Church herself.'

The orchard cemetery or paradise garden

'Thy plants are a paradise…with the fruits of the orchard' (*Sg* 4:13).

Christians have interpreted the Song as an allegory of Christ's love for His bride, the Church, or of His love for the individual soul. In that sense, the Paradise garden reflected the place where each one would eventually find true happiness and fulfilment in the eternal love of the Beloved. This garden, which also included flowers, was found in the area directly behind the High altar and symbolized the transition between earthly and eternal life. One suspects that the planting of fruit trees was deliberately based on the earlier-quoted texts from Revelation. Here, the monks and nuns must have prayed that the deceased members of their communities would eventually have access to the 'New Jerusalem' and enjoy the fruit of the 'tree of life'.

These ideas can be suggested in your own garden by having a fruit tree and bed(s) of flowers appropriate to the remembrance of your own beloved dead and of those more famous who have helped, and still accompany your spiritual journey. As examples, I have a **Clematis** named after Blessed John Paul II, (which bloomed on the morning I left for his beatification in Rome) and clumps of Marguerite and Sweet William for my parents. And the slightly fragrant red **floribunda Rose 'Remembrance'**, is ideal not just for our war dead but for all the souls in

Purgatory. As for fruit trees, nowadays many semi-standard and dwarf varieties overcome problems of space and extensive root systems. I have productive cherry and apple trees planted directly in the earth of my liturgical garden, and Olive, Vine and Fig (perhaps the most 'biblical' of plants) growing successfully in large pots in the courtyard next to the house.

Sacristan's garden

This too was usually found towards the east, with easy access to the Sacristy and flower rooms for the gathering and preparation of flowers for the church. It is a lovely idea to have a special bed or border in your garden that will keep your parish church sanctuary supplied throughout all liturgical seasons.

Herb gardens

The herbs in these gardens could also be found in the cloister garth or courtyards next to the church.

The Physic or Apothecary's garden

This was often located, as was the Infirmary which it served, to the north eastern end of the complex, It was usually quite a large area featuring pathways which divided a series of raised beds each growing a different medicinal herb. The monastic habit of planting different subjects in clearly demarcated squares was particularly important in a medicinal garden, given the differing effects they had on the human system. Some were dangerous if not administered in a carefully controlled dosage. (Ellis Peters' well-researched Brother Cadfael novels frequently show how important this was).

The Kitchen garden

Some vegetables were grown here but this garden seems to have specialised in the provision of culinary herbs so that there would be a continual and plentiful supply, particularly of the more common ones such as mint, thyme and parsley.

The Cloister and garth

'My sister, my spouse is a garden enclosed
The fountain of gardens: the well of living waters' (*Sg* 4:15).
'Cloister' means an enclosed space, and 'garth' is an early word for garden.

The hidden, spiritual life of the monastic community was symbolised by this four-sided roofed walkway, looking inward towards its central space. It was usually built of stone onto to the side of the church, the northern cloister giving direct access to the monks' choir and stalls. The intention was not to imprison the monks, but to protect them from the intrusion and distraction of 'the world' outside. As with many other aspects of monastery gardens, the Cloister and garth had a spiritual significance as well as a practical effect.

At first the garth consisted of finely cut grass with a central fountain calling to mind the 'well of life'. Moreover, the square motif, although having its origins in ancient Roman gardens, is also an important feature in the monastic style of planting individual plots, as a means of dividing different plant species from one another.

'Obedientiary' gardens

These were the private gardens of the Abbot and other senior members of the monastic community. They seem to have been places for relaxation or entertaining guests, adorned with trellises bearing roses and other sweet scented climbing plants. Perhaps they were called 'obedientiary' gardens because the rest of the community gardened them under the vow of obedience. You will most likely want an area for relaxation in your garden, but unless you can afford a gardener, you will have to do the work yourself!

Symbolism, astrology and cosmic considerations

These factors were important in the medieval mind. Plants had different meanings or associations and they were planted for that reason, as well as for their usefulness in the Infirmary or kitchen. Either they had the names of saints (**Herb Peter**, **Herb Bennet**, respectively the **Cowslip** and **Avens**) or Angels (the **dead nettle Yellow Archangel**). They drew attention to a virtue (**Chaste Tree**, or **Monk's Pepper** used as a condiment because it was found to suppress libido); to a particular hour of the Office (**Vesper Flower** which releases its sweetest scent in the late afternoon); or to legend (**Dog Rose**, Legend of St Dorothy one of several patrons of Gardeners). The belief was firmly held that all life forms, including plants, were influenced by Astrology. Plants ruled by Jupiter were thought to be excellent in nature. In creating their gardens, the monks may well have considered the ruling planet of each plant.

Perhaps this seems ridiculous to our sophisticated modern sensibilities. In fact, the monks not only explored the boundaries of knowledge in their search for truth, but in the process, they depicted a miniature Cosmos in their gardens.

We may have wider and more exact knowledge, but we owe respect and gratitude to our ancestors in faith for having led the way, and should echo their wonder and awe at God's total creation. In fact Pope Benedict XVI has often made reference to his deeply reasoned Theology of the Cosmos, one that inspires in humanity a true and realistic vision of itself in relation to its Cosmic Creator. The medieval reasoning behind the use of certain plants was indeed far-fetched, but let us not forget that many of them were effective, and are still used in the manufacture of proprietary drugs, **Valerian**, **Blessed Thistle** and **Foxglove** for instance. Others such as **Calendula** and **Arnica** provide reliable remedies in modern homeopathic medicine. The sap of **Aloe Vera** is so powerful in the treatment of burns that it is stock-piled by several governments in case of nuclear war.

The lore of plants

The lore of plants is a treasury of verifiable history and of legend and custom, some of which has its roots in the pre-Christian era. The Church is known to have absorbed the pagan Winter and Spring Solstices as Christmas and Easter, but to assume that she merely appropriated previous rituals and practices is surely to look at history through the wrong end of the telescope. What the Church did goes much deeper than that.

The **Holly** for instance was sacred to the Druids and the Pagans had sprinkled their newborn babies with Holly water. It was supposed to ward off evil and destruction and was associated with eternity, perhaps because of its long-lived berries and affirmation of life during mid-winter dormancy. The practice is so reminiscent of Christian Baptism as to suggest, not that the Church imitated former practice, but that the Pagans had groped blindly for the Sacrament that God would reveal in His own good time. It is as if our ancestors knew by instinct that they had need of it, but could only continue to sprinkle their infants with that powerless Holly water, until Christ, through His vivifying Spirit, came to give us the Holy water of Sacramental Baptism. I make no excuse for taking symbolism and legend into account, which without Christian transmutation and interpretation would remain as mere superstition and fairy-tale. Similarly, to omit the experience of medieval monastics from our consideration, is to ignore a huge chronological chunk of the Christian gardener's history and acquisition of knowledge. As orthodox believers we do not worship the plants themselves but rather allow them to stimulate our worship of God.

French Cure's gardens

These are still found near the church or in the Presbytery grounds in many country parishes in France. They vary in size, grandeur and formality but all are based on the principle of the square, the plot being divided into four with a well or pond at the centre, thus echoing the traditional monastic garth. As a whole they combine the purposes of all the separate monastery gardens, providing food for the Cure, flowers for the altar of his church, healing plants for his medicine cabinet and a quiet and private place where he could meditate and pray his Breviary. With the decline in priestly vocations and reduction in French Mass attendance, many presbyteries have been sold. Fortunately quite a few are in the hands of keen private gardeners who are interested in their maintenance and history.

Some traditional monastic herbs

Most are perennial; *A/B* denotes annual/biennial plants. *C* = culinary; *M* = medicinal; *S* =sensory *SWU* = Still widely used.

Alexanders *C* Used in a Lenten soup as an antidote to too much salted fish!

Borage *AB SWU* Cooling opening and cleansing, raises the spirits, meaning - Courage.

Chamomile *MCS SWU* creeping ground cover; used against weariness, fever, headaches, Signifies humility.

Chives *C SWU*.

Comfrey *M* used in the setting of broken bones.

Fennel *CMS SWU* Used to treat eye or digestive problems; meaning clear sightedness.

Feverfew *M* for calming fever, has recently gained popularity as a migraine treatment.

English lavender *MS SWU* for calming the nerves, a medieval strewing herb; connections in legend with the Virgin Mary. (See section 'Marian Gardens')

Lemon Balm *SM* rivals the Dock as an effective relief for nettle and other stings. Applied to an affected area of skin the leaf seems to draw out the poison, turning the leaf brown.

Lovage *CS*.

Marjoram (oregano) *C SWU*.

Mint *CS SWU.*

Nasturtium *C* Used as a condiment.

Parsley *C SWU* Good for the digestion, long associated with feasting.

Rosemary *CS SWU* Long known as the 'Herb of Grace', or of remembrance, and associated with Our Lady, but not because of its English name, which in fact is a corruption of the Latin 'Rosmarinus', literally meaning 'dew of the sea', Even to this day you may hear the old saying. 'Where Rosemary flourishes best, you can hear the sea.' According to legend the flowers became miraculously blue when Mary cast her cloak over a Rosemary bush during the flight of the Holy Family into Egypt.

Sage *CM SWU* Good as an internal and external cleansing agent and long synonymous with Immortality.

Thyme *CMS SWU.*

Winter Savory *CM* like many monastic herbs savory is good for the digestion and was probably grown as a healthy addition to the diet. The recipe for Green Chartreuse, although still a secret, apparently calls for over a hundred different herbs, to produce a liqueur in which no one flavour predominates although the presence of several can be detected by flavour and scent. It is the best digestive I know.

Yarrow *M* Used for staunching the flow of blood from wounds Also known as Soldier's Woundwort.

Modern prayer gardens

Both privately and publicly there seems to be increased interest today and many Retreat Centres have incorporated a quiet enclosed garden where their guests can find the quiet seclusion that is supportive of prayer and reflection.[4]

In continuity with ancient monastic principles, modern Prayer gardens are often themed or set forth a narrative through the symbolism and positioning of plants and other features.

Creation gardens

These are gardens where the entire space is devoted to the representation of the first two chapters of Genesis. Unless your garden is fairly large and has variety in its natural contours the necessary landscaping may put this idea beyond possibility, but such a garden can witness to your ecological concerns and foster the adoption of practices that preserve God's creation, not only in the sense described above, but also by encouraging you to look for plants that have become increasingly rare through pollution, destruction of meadowland, and modern chemical control of wild flowers.[5]

A Jericho rockery – (based on Jos 6)

This garden can be less ambitious. You may wish to search for appropriately named rock plants and alpines, but the larger significance of your Jericho site will be deeply personal and hidden. If you already have a rockery, it may help you to think of it as representing a tumbled down wall. Indeed this thought will be encouraged if you decide to build a rockery, for when all its stones are assembled on the chosen spot, they will very much resemble a fallen wall, calling to mind the breach through which the Israelites gained access to the Promised Land. In fact and in symbol, the wall denotes defence and protection, or indeed imprisonment, but for those outside it may signify division and exclusion, or freedom. But with apologies to a favourite American poet, before I built a rockery:

> 'I'd ask to know
> What I was walling in or walling out
> And to whom I was like to give offence'
> (Robert Frost's *'Mending Wall'*).

Either as individuals or nations, we build walls for several reasons. Your Jericho rockery can lead to meditation on which walls we have built either physically or spiritually, and why.

Catechesis and retreat gardens

Here, plants are deliberately laid out and labelled, in beds, borders or arbours that assist the teaching of points in the Catechism or lead to reflection on particular themes of a retreat programme. They are chosen because of their traditional meaning and associations, or because of the significance given them in the Victorian Language of Flowers.[6]

Others are included as the result of the gardener director's personal insights. Several trees would be desirable and if space is at a premium, audio visual aids, including the Internet, are fruitful resources and particularly helpful when the weather is inclement.

Sample Catechesis beds

Fruits or the Holy Spirit: Charity – Vine, Turnip; Joy – Crocus, Queen Anne's Lace; Peace – 'Peace' Rose; Patience – Leek, Dock; Benignity – Grapes of the Vine; Goodness – All Good; Longanimity – Bamboo; Faith – Lychnis, Bluebell, Veronica, Ground Ivy, Plum Tree; Modesty – Columbine, Marjoram; Continency – Azalea; Chastity – Thistle, Tansy.

The Four Last Things: Death – Hemlock, Arum Lily; Judgment – Rudbeckia; Hell – Devil's Bit(e) Scabious; Heaven – Tree of Life, Tree of Heaven (Ailanthus), Everlasting Sweet Pea, Amaranth and Sage all signify eternal life.

A Bower of Beatitudes

The poor in spirit – Sweet Chestnut (Poverty).

The meek - Birch Tree (Meekness).

Those who mourn - Aloe Vera, Harebell (Grief and Sorrow), Snowdrop (Consolation).

The hungry and thirsty after justice - Horse Chestnut (Justice).

The merciful - Elder, Allspice (compassion), Dwarf Pine (Pity), Juniper (God's Mercy).

The pure in heart - Water Lily, Star-of-Bethlehem.

The peacemakers - 'Peace' Rose, Olive.

The persecuted for the sake of justice - Snakeshead Lily.

St Benedict's retreat – basic outline

The vows

Stability – Thuya plicata – On a physical level the vow binds the monk or nun to a specific house, but metaphorically it clearly applies to Oblates and other lay affiliates of different monasteries.

Conversion of manners – Rose 'Metanoia'.

The promise to embrace Chastity– (Monk's Pepper – Vitex agnus-castus, Tansy, Willowherb) and **Poverty** (Vernal Grass, Wood Anemone).

Obedience – Traditionally symbolised by Broom, possibly because of its pliant branches.

Life and works which lead to the study of
The Rule of Saint Benedict

The 'Opus Dei' – Indoor Prayer Plant (*Maranta leuconeura*) All Benedictines should daily, in community, recite or preferably sing, the full Divine Office. It is the universal prayer of the Church, her work for God.

'Lectio Divina' – Bulrush (*Scirpus lacustris* can be tricky to manage in a domestic pond but is available for purchase already dried) symbolises the written word of God (see *Is* 19:7 and *Ezk* 3:3). The prophet's literal and spiritual consumption of the 'scroll' prefigures the Benedictine daily time immersed in the prayerful study of the Scriptures and other spiritual reading.

Manual labour – Bee Orchis, Flax (industriousness and hard work). The Benedictine day balances spiritual and intellectual pursuits with physical work.

Hospitality – When found together Oak and Holly traditionally represent this particular Benedictine welcome to strangers and pilgrims, rich and poor alike.

Arts and architecture – Acanthus and Candytuft respectively. A proper study of Benedictine/Cistercian contribution in these areas would yield sufficient materials for a whole series of retreats.

Education – The Cherry Tree (Good Education). The lives of many saints demonstrate the Benedictine/Cistercian thirst to acquire and disseminate knowledge in the service and glory of God.

Love – Philadelphus (Fraternal Love). The Brothers must truly love each other, whatever their individual faults of body or soul.

Ten Benedictine and Cistercian Saints

SS Maurus and Placid (6th Century) – Hollyhock symbolises fruitfulness chosen in acknowledgement of Maurus' fruitful labour in south west France.

SS Cedd and Chad (7th Century) – Candytuft traditionally signifies architecture and is chosen for these blood brothers to commemorate the monasteries they built, and to Chad as founder of the See of Lichfield.

St Benet Biscop (7th century) – Bear's Breeches represents the Arts, and appropriate to a saint who brought so much music and painting from the continent to enhance the liturgy in his native Britain.

And from the early 12th century

St Wulstan – Water Lily - signifies eloquence and is given to this native of Warwickshire because of articulacy in his native Anglo-Saxon.

SS Alberic, Robert of Molesme, Stephen Harding – Holy Thistle (*Cnicus benedictus*) has a traditional significance of austerity and independence and is therefore suitable for men who displayed both in their foundation and observance a stricter form of Benedictinism.

St Aelred – Monk's Rhubarb – once believed helpful in the treatment of gallstones, from which we know that St Aelred suffered.

Marian gardens

Before the Reformation, many plants were attributed to Our Lady because of their names. By their names and by the Marian legends associated with them. Familiar examples survive to this day in names such as 'Maidenhair Fern', 'Maiden Pink', 'Lily of the Valley' and 'Marigold'. 'Lady's Mantle', and innumerable others have names that denote them as belonging to some unidentified historical, or romantically idealised lady. All of these would have originally been known to our ancestors as plants of **Our Lady**, the now missing word having been lost or discouraged as Marian devotion waned during the centuries following the Protestant reform. However, the children of 'Our Lady's Dowry' have never forgotten this fact, or have recently been delighted to discover it and have increasingly included many of Mary's plants in gardens especially dedicated to her. A long border or alley is suitable to walk along as you pray and a circular Rosary bed invites you to walk round it as you meditate its Mysteries, mirroring as it does, the shape of the Rosary Beads when laid on a flat surface.

Through the year with Our Lady

December

Immaculate Conception – Gallica 'Rosa Mundi' Introduced before 1500, slightly fragrant; pale pink striped crimson; Almond (signifies Virgin Birth).

Nativity Christmas Rose; Lady's Bedstraw (Ground cover).

Holy Family/flight into Egypt (within the Christmas Octave) – Lavender because of the legend that the Virgin Mary, looking for somewhere to hang her Baby's clothes, draped them on a lavender bush, which until then had been scentless. After she took in her laundry, the bush was imbued with the wonderful perfume that it keeps to this day. A similar legend attaches to Rosemary.

January

Mother of God – Marigold (Mary Gold or Mary Bud), Annual, height to 20 inches; Our Lady's Milk Herb (Lungwort); Marys Thistle (Milk Thistle); Star-of-Bethlehem (Virgin's Milk); Motherwort (St Mary's Hand); Mother of God's Tea (White Horehound).

February

Candlemas – Box (Purification plant), Snow Drop (aka Candlemas Bell, Lady's Taper, Eve's Tears).

Finding in the Temple Mary's Gloves (Foxglove).

Our Lady of Lourdes – Climbing fragrant gold repeat flowering rose 'Golden Showers'. (A single golden rose rested on each of the Blessed Virgin's feet during the Apparitions at Lourdes.); *Saxifrage oppositifolium*, early ground cover, flowers pinkish purple in March (Apparently the plant eaten by Bernadette during the 9th Apparition).

March

The Annunciation Madonna Lily.

Mary's month of May

Help of Christians – Wood Sorrel represents Maternal Tenderness.

Pentecost – Climbing Rose 'Danse du Feu' (red orange blooms, repeat flowering, virtually scentless) and Anemone (aka Windflower).

Visitation – The Iris has an ancient symbolism of faith, wisdom, courage and eloquence; four qualities demonstrated by Our Lady and Elizabeth during this event. In Flemish Art it rivals the lily for the title 'Flower of the Holy Virgin.

June

Immaculate Heart of Mary (moveable Memoria, Saturday after Sacred Heart) – Dicentra (in French 'Mary's Heart'). Pink heartshaped flowers April to early June hanging from arching stems. Height 30 inches, spread two feet.

July

Mount Carmel – Terebinth Tree.

SS Joachim and Anne (Our Lady's parents) – Clematis 'Happy Marriage'.

August

Mary Major – Our Lady of the snows – Motherwort; Rose 'Virgo Rose' to commemorate the white snow of petals that traditionally fall from Mary Major's ceiling on this day.

Assumption – Lily of the Valley.

Queenship (Coronation) – Mary's Glory (Saint John's Wort); Meadowsweet (Queen of the Meadows); Our Lady's Cushion (Thrift); Rose 'Gracious Queen' (Hybrid tea, medium yellow).

September

Birthday – Pennyroyal (Our Lady's Birthday Flower), 'Little Mary' (Blue-eyed grass, 'Bellum Ministrum').

Sorrows – Lady's Tears (Virginian Spiderwort); White Patio Rose 'Tear Drop'.

Walsingham (formerly of Ransom) – Lady's Purse (Slipper Wort) to commemorate the famous Slipper Chapel; Costmary.

October (Mary's month)

Rosary – Lady's Fingers (Honeysuckle).

November

Presentation – Our Lady's Needlework (London Pride) Lady's Tresses (Maidenhair Fern); Smock (Cuckoo Flower); Lady's Frills (Primrose), Mantle (Alchemilla), Mary's Shawl (Sage); Slippers (Monkshood) Our Lady's Cushion (Thrift).

To complete a circular Rosary bed

Baptism of Christ – Water (or land) Cress; Baptisia.

Proclamation of Gospel – Rose 'Good News' (Medium Yellow fragrant floribunda).

Transfiguration – Rose 'White Cloud' White exceptionally fragrant climber); Sunflower (annual).

Eucharist – Rose 'Remember Me' (Coral to Yellow fragrant Hybrid Tea).

Events of the Lord's Passion – Judas Tree, Pasque Flower, Passionflower, Aloe Vera.

Crowning with Thorns

Crucifixion – Elder.

Resurrection – Easter Lilies (*Lilium Longiflorum*); Arum Lily (Latin mane in TFL).

Marian hedging and edging

'Rosarie de l'Hay' Rose Rugosa, fragrant wine-red blooms, bushy repeat flowerer, height up to 6-7 feet will grow on poor soil and in exposed conditions. Juniper (Madonna's Bush), Rosemary (Our Lady as Star of the Sea), and Lavender (Help of Christians).

Basic garden tasks and prayer

Every garden is potentially a place of prayer.

'Whether we are gardening or appreciating the results of our own or someone else's labour, we are reflecting the active and contemplative life. A gardener must be a 'Martha' busy about many things, but Mary's 'better part' is always there for the choosing. Indeed it is possible to balance the two, so that the first is absorbed into the second, as the Benedictines have been demonstrating for centuries. As Kipling reminds us –'Oh Adam was a gardener, and God who made him sees/ That half a proper gardener's work is done upon his knees.' A great deal of the other half, in my experience, is spent doubled over in a frequently painful attitude of submission. Both praying and gardening demand discipline, stamina and consistency. In either activity, an hour's daily attention will yield a more abundant harvest than if one goes at it in an excess of enthusiasm for several days and then neglects it for weeks. The attempt to gain control over weeds in the garden, or in the soul, is a life-long business. As believers, we turn to prayer in all experience – happy, sad, or harsh – and through all rites of passage – joyful, solemn, or anguished. As praying gardeners, we find the garden a celebratory place in the good times, and a therapeutic, even cathartic one in the bad.

Gardening is supportive of prayer because it stimulates our thanksgiving to God; it makes us more keenly aware of His presence; it stirs our desire to praise His eternal creativity and constantly renews our awe of His power. Moreover it does not inspire these forms of prayer only at harvest time or when we rejoice to see the brave snowdrops begin to pierce the earth, or behold the perfection of the first rose of summer. When we are tending our plants with close concern, it is difficult not to be pleasurably astonished by their intricacy and delicacy, their variety and beauty of form, scent and colour. How is it possible to adore and glorify the design and not the Designer? I am one happy gardener when I find myself praying in these ways whilst actually working or simply observing in my plot. Gardening teaches patience, and to pray for it when we lack it, not simply because of various time-consuming tasks and the extended growing periods of some subjects, but because sometimes we simply cannot afford to buy the plants we want. There is always something on a gardener's 'wish list'! As present-giving times approach always ask your fellow-gardeners what they would like to receive.

Even basic garden activities can lend themselves to different types of prayer. For example: *ground clearance*, *digging* and other repetitive rhythmic tasks invite one to prayers of the same nature, the Rosary for instance, and because the work at hand is in itself quite tedious and boring, it leaves the mind relatively empty and inactive, thus making it possible to offer the prayers with greater concentration and devotion. I know my garden intimately and that to dig one potato trench affords me time to pray a decade of the Rosary. If the work is particularly arduous it can be offered up as a physical penance, remembering God's decree to Adam that he should till the earth with toil. When physical demands have seemed beyond my strength I have always kept going with repetition of the Jesus prayer separating, its phrases with every new thrust of spade or mattock. 'Jesus Christ Son of the Living God have mercy on me a sinner'.

Over the years I have come to associate *weeding* with awareness of sin, and real sorrow for it. A session with the hoe or of rooting up the unwanted invaders by hand becomes an opportunity for the examination of conscience and preparation for the Sacrament of Penance. As already mentioned when *sowing*, *planting*, *pruning* and *mowing* the actions can stimulate spontaneous meditation on one of the many appropriate biblical texts, particularly from the Gospels.

Sometimes the joyful sense of purpose I feel in the garden spills out in *song*. 'Fight the Good fight', 'He who would Valiant be' and 'My faith it is an Oaken Staff' are frequent favourites for energetic work. For gentler tasks much loved Plainchant comes automatically to the vocal chords, - *'Ubi Caritas'* for instance or the Benediction hymns and Marian Latin hymns.

The praying gardener's God given bonuses

Whether 'making a joyful noise unto the Lord' or meditating silently, whether praying freely or to a formula, I have found that the concentration takes the mind from physical discomfort and ensures that the work is completed with increased thoroughness, and at a steady pace not exceeding wisdom. And yet in spite of this, the ground seems to be covered more quickly than if the time had been spent thinking about next week's shopping list, or what you would do if you won the lottery.

Gardening sharpens the physical and spiritual senses

This is particularly true in a Herb Garden – so many different perfumes from the clean astringency of southernwood to the delicate sweetness of woodruff, and the scents of lemon balm and lemon grass differ subtly from one another. Nothing demonstrates so clearly that green is not one colour; it is as many colours as there are subjects growing there. Urban living may so deaden our sense of hearing that gardens can initially seem to be very silent places. But at dawn and dusk particularly in spring and summer, the birds make them jubilantly noisy. The more time one spends in the garden, the more one's ear becomes attuned to the glorious variety of bird-call and song, and to the different noises made by insects and small mammals among the plants. The great black beetle begins to sound as if he's wearing hiking boots, and here in France, out of the corner of my ear I can hear a lizard darting into its home under the stones of Our Lady's grotto. One summer morning I discovered that an army of squashy, shiny red grubs, the size of five pence pieces, had invaded my potato patch, and I could only watch in astonished panic as they swarmed over the plants. But what amazed and horrified me even more was that I could actually hear them munching their way through the leaves. Conversely, the absence of human prattle and noise in the garden makes for the kind of silence that Pope Benedict has taught as being essential to prayer (eg. *General Audience Catechesis* 7th March 2012).

Learning from the hard times

Gardening is definitely not all harmony, progress and jubilation and as in the spiritual life we learn not to look for short cuts and quick results. At the very least both gardening and prayer teach patience and courage. Even so there will be times when we become daunted by the sheer hard work involved and find difficulty in beginning, let alone completing it. There are times of drought, disappointment, anxiety and disease. We, and the garden, are parched and barren; the seed refuses to germinate. After an hour's prayer or gardening we seem to have achieved nothing, heard nothing, felt nothing. There is no consolation. All is dark, cold and unproductive. Prayer and labour have become burdensome fruitless chores. And yet at other times some pest (like the nasty potato grub), kills the plants, decimates a crop, and gnaws at the soul. 'If only I make more effort and work hard enough', we say to ourselves, 'things are bound to improve.' Of course we should labour diligently and have good intentions, but our wretched human insistence on being in control dictates that we cannot be at peace until *we* have rooted out the problem through our own efforts alone. We forget that without God we can do nothing and that only His grace, mercy and power can lighten the darkness, send the rain, heal the disease, and enable us, and our plants, to develop. When the clouds break at the end of a difficult time in prayer or gardening, they do so at His behest, not ours, and we realise anew that progress is not something *we* make. It is done *to* us and *for* us, not by us. As the darkness disperses we feel ourselves plucked out of the slough and are drawn onward and upward to the next stage of growth, just as we find one morning that the precious green of slow germinating parsley has at last spiked its way towards the light.

Intercession

Gardening is often solitary and can lead to introspection and self-absorption. I often use my plants to remind me to pray for others. On Saints days I visit the plants that commemorate them, and pray for parish communities, hospitals schools and other Church institutions who have that particular saint as patron. During your research into the history and folklore of plants you will be led by each one, to intercession for different groups of people, for the needs of particular individuals and for those of the universal Church. I promise you that this works in every case.

For instance during the first week of Advent **Fennel** inspires the following Intercessions: 'For the poor and starving; for those suffering from eating disorders; for nursing mothers and their babies; for those who work in industries where Fennel is used; for the physically blind; for eye specialists and opticians; for improvement in human stewardship of the planet and the conservation of wildlife; for beekeepers and conservationists; for the people of France and Italy.

For the spiritually blind and desolate; for an increase in faith; for strength and steadfastness in prayer; for grace to resist the temptation to physical or spiritual sloth; for the fortitude to carry our cares'.

The little session ends with a reading from Longfellow and a thanksgiving for poets and artists whose works sharpen our perceptions and insights.

'Above the lower plants it towers,
The fennel with its golden flowers,
And in an earlier age than ours
Was gifted with the wondrous powers
Lost vision to restore.'

Warning: Fennel is deeply tap-rooted and an eager self-seeder. Unless you want a fennel forest, root out the inevitable seedlings round your plant before they are 3 inches tall. Indeed I would say it is second only to grass and the daisy in its indestructibility. Not surprisingly does it represent strength of faith in our folk lore.

The Divine Office

Readers who pray the Liturgy of the Hours and do not have easy access to church or chapel may have already discovered, from the first burst of spring until Autumn gives way to winter, the joy of joining the universal prayer of the Church in their garden, and if not, I cannot recommend it highly enough. It is a great privilege to be able to say the morning Office in the sunlit dawn garden. It is so easy in such surroundings to be in accord with the psalmist's outpouring of joy and praise: 'The pastures of the wilderness drip, the hills gird themselves with joy, the meadows clothe themselves with flocks, the valleys deck themselves with grain, they shout and sing together for joy' (*Ps* 65:12-13). Being able to see and hear the birds lends special significance and profound awareness as one prays the verse: 'Even the sparrow finds a home, and the swallow a nest for herself, where she may lay her young, at thy altars, O Lord of hosts, my king and my God' (*Ps* 84:3). One blessedly happy summer morning in the early 90s, I was reading Lauds before beginning my day's work in the garden. Suddenly I was overcome with such love for the Word of God, which was veritably alive in my hands and was being allowed to come out of my mouth, that I had to stop. Literally it took my breath away and I have never forgotten it. Many times since, it has helped me through periods of aridity and anxiety, the love I felt on that original occasion has continued to deepen and grow over the intervening years, and has enriched my participation in the Liturgy of the Word at Mass. The Office Readings and Antiphons fit as perfectly into the Lectionary as does a soundly-made tenon into its mortise. Of course, I could have had such an experience anywhere, but the fact remains that it happened during prayer in my garden.

My garden of the liturgy

'Let the favour of the Lord our God be upon us, and prosper for us the work of our hands!' (*Ps* 90:17).

Gardening had always borne spiritual fruit for me. I had gardened in south Devon for many years when suddenly I had to leave that beloved county and return to live and work in central London. During the gardenless decade that followed I began to dream of one day making a garden for God and this dream eventually began to materialise when we bought this house in south west France, a region that I describe geographically as 'Devon writ-large'. My mother and I grew a lot of potatoes in those days because they have the effect of cleaning the ground, not due to some magical property special to them, but because at every stage of their growth, from first digging to final lifting and clearance, the earth requires close and constant attention. At this point vegetables took up most of the available time and space and as yet I had no clear idea of an overall theme for the plot.

I did however put in the Thuya hedges and designed an enclosed herb garden. I planted a bay tree on either side of an archway of 'Paul's Scarlet' roses which form its entrance. '*Laurus*', the Latin name for Bay, means 'triumph', and I chose them as a sign of my prayer that God would crown my efforts with success. To this day, every time I pass between them, that prayer is offered, and unfailingly, they remind me that it is God who gives me a sense of purpose, protection determination and strength. During any spare time, whether in London or France, I researched avidly into the lore, history and nomenclature of plants. I was struck by the frequency with which Christian association occurred and began to wonder whether it would be possible to make a garden where most plants would have a specific spiritual meaning or biblical significance.

And now each spring, as an integral part of my joy in Our Lord's Resurrection, I celebrate the opening of yet another Season of close friendship with the garden I have since made with God's help and oversight. It wasn't until my retirement that I was able to live here permanently but sadly by then, because of priest and people shortage, our village church had lost its Sunday Mass and was only used for funerals and rare marriages. Even the Angelus bell was silent and apparently irreparable. But as the years have passed that garden has proved a constant companion during the vicissitudes of life. It shared my happiness in the good times and was a balm to my spirit when in deep grief and paralysing anxiety. Most of all though during that period of sacramental dearth in the village, it was through the garden that God sustained and showered me with His gifts of faith, hope, fortitude and love. Let Him be eternally worshipped and thanked!

Well before my retirement I had reached the point

where I was gardening with God as well as for Him and one effect was spilling over into the rest of my spiritual and practical life. Thus He led me 'in the right paths for his name's sake'. And then in the herb garden one sunlit May morning, I realised that it *was* possible to make the kind of garden I had envisaged long ago. Over the following weeks the outline of a new spiritual map for the garden began to unfold. I only had to listen, watch, and follow. Originally the long, flat rectangular plot (150 x 30 feet) had been divided into four. Now I saw that it must have six, clearly separate areas and knew from research and study that there existed more than enough plants to inhabit them and 'speak' their different spiritual messages. Eventually to walk round the whole would be to follow the Church's liturgical year both physically and spiritually. It would in fact be a 'living' Divine Office, a 'green' monastery. On that May morning I estimated that about five years work lay ahead before the new plan became a reality. My forecast having proved accurate; the following had taken shape in reality by the time I retired from London to France.

My garden layout

(1) Advent, Christmastide and Pre-Lent 'Chapel' – enclosed by impenetrable 'walls' of climbing plants and trees. Densely populated with subjects suggesting themes and saints of the season, it is dominated by the Apple Tree representing Jesus and the light of the

Incarnation. On the eastern side is the pond having a three-fold significance: first as the River Jordan of Christ's Baptism, second as the place of our own Baptism, and thirdly as the well where Our Lord met the Woman of Samaria. A statue of her is at its brink, standing for ourselves before our own first encounter with the Lord and indeed for the entire Church.

(2) The Lenten chapter bed and pleached Way of the Cross. These are found to the left of an archway from 1 above. Here grow subjects that are a stimulus to Lenten prayer and practice. At the far end of the Chapter Bed there is a clump of Madonna lily for the Annunciation. Then turning right one enters the Way of the Cross, constructed as a 12 section pergola. This runs the length of the west side of the garden its arches and climbing plants, providing seclusion from eastern and western view. At its northernmost end, the Twelfth Station is marked by the Passion Flower growing over the Archway leading to the Sanctuary of the Passion and Resurrection.

(3) The Sanctuary of the Passion and Resurrection At its western side is the Cross on a slight rise of stones, and made from two discarded old beams. The rest of this little enclosure suggests the burial garden of Jesus and in the far eastern corner a trellis arbour represents His empty tomb. A statue of the Sacred Heart on the north boundary looks south between the bay trees. Passing between them, on the left one comes to:

(4) Our Lady's Grotto of Pentecost and the pilgrim pathway of Spring and high Summer, the latter running along the eastern boundary of the plot. (Opposite her Immaculate Heart statue in the grotto is a small rose garden).

(5) At the south-eastern corner one comes to the **Autumn arbour of the Angels and repose of remembrance**. Before leaving via the Advent 'Chapel' and its gated eastern exit, you can look back and inspect or harvest anything that is ripe in the central garth of nourishment and healing.

(6) Central garth of nourishment and healing. This is surrounded on all four sides by the areas and features outlined in 1- 5 above.

The **Obedientary courtyard** was not established until the first years after my retirement and permanent residence here and is accessed directly from the French windows of my study. It is enclosed on the south, west and north by the house and other domestic buildings, and on the east by boundary hedges and fencing. It is a sunny protected area and has a small kitchen plot of the most frequently used herbs. Here, a statue of St Francis presides over a little orchard. (Elder – 'The Medicine chest of the poor', Vine, Olive, Fig, Apricot, and strawberries. And in the sunniest, most secluded spot (enclosed on three sides) St Therese protects her own Rose Arbour.

Choosing plants

In many cases plants 'self-seed, so to speak, and are chosen because they are mentioned in the Bible, or for their names, structure, characteristics, or meaning in folk-lore or the nineteenth century language of flowers. And so we have for instance, **Spanish Bayonet** (Yucca) for Saint Ignatius of Loyola, **Trillium** for the Holy Trinity, **Chamomile** for humility, **Borage** for courage; **Snakeshead Lily** for persecution, the **Madonna Lily** for the Annunciation and Honesty (Pope's Pennies) for the intentions of our Holy Father. I chose the **Red Clover** for Saint Hilary of Poitiers because of his treatise '*De Trinitate*', an extract from which forms the second reading in the Divine Office for his feast day. And **All Heal** for perhaps the best known patron saint of gardeners, the 7th century Irish monk who studied the medicinal properties of plants, founded a monastery near Meaux and was one of the most successful and sought-after healers of his day.

Appropriately named varieties

You may discover an appropriately named variety when leafing through garden reference books and catalogues. My two **'Metanoia' roses** were found in this way, one for all Benedictines and the other for St Ephraem of Syria. In 2007 I marked Pope Benedict's '*Summorum Pontificum*' with the **patio rose 'Mozart'**. For Frances of Rome, I found the **Narcissus 'Angel'**, ideal for this saint of practical charity who is well known for her extended series of visions of her guardian angel.

Liturgical colours

You can also make use of **liturgical colours** in your design. As the Church clothes herself and her priests, so will your garden reflect the seasons as they turn – violet in Advent and Lent, white for Our lady's feasts and Virgin Saints, rose pink for Gaudete and Laetare Sundays and so on.

An obvious choice can inspire a deeper meditation

It is astonishing how frequently **obvious choices** provide springboards to quite lengthy meditation; and often the humbler the plant, the deeper reflection it stimulates. A prime example of this occurred when I decided on the **'Star of Bethlehem'**, (*Ornithogalum*) for **Epiphany**, and which led me to an unexpectedly week-long meditation and prayer. Apart from its name, there are other reasons why this flower is so suitable. It is shy and has to be searched for in the wild, but is delightful when found, thus symbolising the long journey of the Magi and their eventual finding of Christ, who is hidden from Herod. Without sufficient sunlight star of Bethlehem will hide its face, much as we are in darkness, until Christ, through His miracle at Cana, lets us glimpse His Light. In the 'language of flowers' the plant represents purity, and reminds us of the purity of Christ and His Mother, and of the cleansing waters of Baptism. The word 'hexandrian' denotes a flower with six stamens was coined by Linnaeus (1707-1778), the Swedish Naturalist, whose work was foundational in the naming of flowers and their component parts. It is this characteristic that turns the Star of Bethlehem into a living marker of the maximum six days of liturgy between the Epiphany and the Baptism of the Lord. It's a good idea to grow a bowl indoors so that if the weather makes the garden chilly, you can study the plant closely and keep warm whilst doing so.

Epiphany of the Lord – January 6

When I contemplate the whole flower, closed or open, and observe its response to light, it will lead me to reflect on the salvation of the whole world manifested in the small child who was visited by the Magi.

First day

The star shape formed by the flower's three petals and three sepals cannot fail to remind me of the star that led the Magi to the Infant Lord of the Universe.

Second day

I concentrate more closely on the way in which the three sepals and three petals surround the six central stamens and think of the petals as symbolic of the Gentiles (as represented by the Magi) and the sepals as the Children of Israel. The shining gold of the stamens reminds me of our hope to behold Christ's glory.

Third day

The three petals or sepals on their own call to mind, not only the symbolism of the Magi's gifts to Christ, but Christ's gifts to each of us. The way we use these gifts will determine the quality of our own humble offerings to Him.

Fourth day

When I hold the seed case in my hand, its six ridges represent the joyful Church, receiving, enclosing, protecting the Seed of the Word and then spreading its Light. With her, I celebrate Epiphanytide each year in a spirit of thanksgiving for the continual Epiphanies Christ makes through the vivifying waters of Baptism and the nourishment of His presence in the Blessed Sacrament.

Fifth day

The six central golden-headed stamens remind me of the Trinitarian aspects of the Epiphany tide liturgy. In it, there are two manifestations for each Person: the Father speaks to the Magi through a dream and then at the Baptism of

Christ; the Son is shown as the Lord of creation and as the Word; the Spirit conceives the Word and witnesses to the divinity Of Christ at His baptism.

Sixth day

As I ponder the way in which the petals and sepals are joined at the centre, I think of the rejoicing Church as she receives the Light of Christ Her Bridegroom; of John the Baptist, her self-described 'best man'; and of the fact that the Lord takes delight in his bride, the pilgrim Church.

Thus a largely disregarded, even plebeian plant, leads so thoroughly into the mysteries of the Epiphany, underlining Christ's lesson, that the greatest shall be least and the least shall be greatest. I love it above all because it led me to an awareness of the history of the Church's emphases during the Epiphany period. The Magi are only a part of it, but even though the liturgy still addresses other aspects of the manifestation of Christ's glory, I think we tend to have neglected them and concentrate mostly on the star and the Kings who followed it. It has also led me to a deeper understanding of Saint Paul's words: 'Great indeed, we confess, is the mystery of our religion: He was manifested in the flesh, vindicated in the Spirit, seen by the angels, preached among the nations, believed on in the world, taken up in glory' (I *Tm* 3:16).

Matching plants to liturgical days and feasts

Sometimes I haven't known until I have studied the life of a saint, the themes of a specific liturgical day or special feast, which plant will match them. **Myrtle**, because of its marriage associations, came in this way for the 17th week of Ordinary Time.

On many other occasions the plant has suggested itself whilst I have actually been dealing with it. This is exemplified by the **Eglantine** for Saint John of the Cross. One day whilst engaged in a pruning battle with it, I thought at first of Chaucer's Prioress, and her rather silly vanities and priorities. Madame Eglantine, with her badge bearing the legend '*Amor vincit omnia*', is concerned with social niceties, manners, accents, and somewhat self-indulgent kindness towards her lap dog and apparently not at all with the spiritual love of the true nun. Chaucer's contemporaries would have immediately appreciated his irony. However the Eglantine is the traditional emblem of poetry itself, and suddenly my eglantine seemed eminently suitable for arguably the greatest poet-mystic that God has raised up in the Church. Moreover, as his appellation suggests, John had a great devotion to the cross and willingly accepted much suffering. The thorns of eglantine reminded me of this. The choice was later reinforced when I found that in his commentary on the Spiritual Canticle, he explains that the Apple Tree represents the cross, and the rose tree the understanding, memory and will of the soul. I did not plant my eglantine. It grew as if from nowhere, close up against my apple tree, making a natural little thicket in that part of the garden. Oh perfect yet unplanned juxtaposition! The second Office Reading for St John's day is from his explanation of lines from the 36th stanza of the Spiritual Canticle, 'Let us enter further into the thicket…'.

Plants may suggest themselves at Church

Other plants may suggest themselves at Church, or in response to paintings, statues and stained glass windows. Until I retired permanently to France, I used to join a tiny Anglo-Catholic congregation who gathered at 7am each morning to recite Matins and Lauds according to the Roman Breviary. Above the altar in the side chapel where the Office was said, there was a stained glass Rose Window, designed and made by Margaret Rope (1891-1988) in memory of a former vicar who had died in 1948. The window depicts 8 of Mary's titles in the Litany of Loreto, including the 'Mystical Rose'. Contemplating this window one morning, I noticed that the stylised rose in that panel was of the old English garden type. This gave me the idea of planting a selection of such roses in celebration of the Immaculate Conception, and eventually led to the composition of a Meditation Prayer entitled '*Rosa Mea*' because in Latin it is a term of endearment and is therefore appropriate when addressing Our Lady whom we love as our mother, as well as honouring her as the Queen of Heaven.[7]

Work colleagues can also inspire a plant choice

In Week 12 of Ordinary Time the liturgy leads us to consider love and friendship. I wanted to remember several friends who have been a rich blessing at different stages of my life. I chose the **Tomato** because of its other name, as the 'Love Apple'. Every late spring and summer when planting, tending and harvesting this reliably abundant crop, I offer thanksgiving and prayer for all those friends, whether they are still living or not. There is, I believe a spiritual element in all close friendships. During the last seven years of my teaching career, I formed a close bond with, one of my work-mates. Of course friendships can founder, often through misunderstanding, or merely through short temper. From time to time in the stresses of school life Margaret* and I offended or annoyed each other, but somehow, at the earliest opportunity after a spat, we would fall over ourselves to admit our own fault and be friends again. Thus in a small way we showed Christ in our lives and deepened our friendship and respect for each other. Nevertheless, the highest, deepest, noblest, most loyal, forgiving and enduring love that humans are capable of bearing toward each other, is a mere shadow of God's love for us. And it is this love above all that the humble tomato helps me to celebrate all the year round.

Spiritual friends, directors and Priests
can inspire plant choice

Sometimes there is such an important development in one's conversations and correspondence with them that certain plants always remind me of a particular friend and insights that we have shared. Thus my three spiritual sisters in Birmingham are always close in the company of **Snowdrops** at Candlemas, or the **Rose 'Compassion'** and the **Pasque flowers** that flourish beneath it in Spring, and the **Forget-me-nots** that one of them sent to me. For another 'adopted' sister who struggles in a parish where individuals oppose the orthodoxy of their priest, I have the **Pomegranate** (bear wrongs patiently), **Balm of Gilead** (forgive injuries), and **Scarlet Geranium** (Comfort of the Sorrowful). For a spiritual director I have the **Passion Flower**. And for the dedicatees of this booklet, the **Rose 'Michel Angelo'**, (Sacred Artistry); **Mulberry tree** (Wisdom), the Heartsease (the Sacred Heart), **Primula 'Mark'** and the **rose 'Rambling Rector'**.

Observation and engagement as a spiritual experience

At yet other times you may through observation and thought, or engagement with a familiar plant, notice something about it that can be turned to spiritual account. Occasionally that engagement may be a spiritual experience in itself, as when I touched a **Snapdragon** at a time when I was searching for a plant to dedicate to **St Thomas** the doubting Apostle. One late September morning, during my daily walk from tube station to school I spotted some mauve-pink snapdragons, escapees from local suburban gardens, growing wild on a patch of waste ground to the side of the road. Having read somewhere that if you gently squeeze the flower, it will open its 'mouth', I decided to experiment. At the very moment of my touching the velvet flower I suddenly remembered the words of Jesus to Saint Thomas, 'Reach out your hand and put it in my side. Do not doubt but believe' (*Jn* 20:27). Sure enough the delicate 'wound' of the flower opened at my touch, and I was so moved that I prayed aloud to Jesus in that deserted spot, echoing Saint Thomas' reply, 'My Lord and my God', words which long ago Sister Agnes had taught me to say at the moments of elevation of Host and Precious Blood at Mass. Then I reflected on Christ's response to Saint Thomas. It is I think, one of His most comforting sayings: 'Have you believed because you have seen me? Blessed are those who have not seen and yet have come to believe' (*Jn* 20:29). That early morning experience carried me with serenity through many of the following days, and does so even now when the memory is unfailingly prompted by the snapdragons in my garden, and as on the original occasion, I experience moments of profound spiritual communion.

Vegetables are rewarding

Every vegetable that I grow makes me think of another patron saint of gardeners, St Phocas of Sinope on the Black Sea. Some records say he was a bishop and others that he was a lay innkeeper. All agree that he gave his surplus garden produce to the poor and that he was martyred by decapitation c. 303, the morning after he had given hospitality to his eventual executioners.

The **Leek** is a willing adaptable servant, as we aim to be in our following of Christ. It is a pale symbol of the dead awaiting resurrection. 'O dwellers in the dust awake and sing for joy' (*Is* 26:19). Leeks reward scrupulous preparatory digging and meticulous planting; in this they mirror a proper preparation for the Lord's coming. As time passes, He continues to cast His influence over the leeks we have set and at the same time constantly nurtures the response we have shown towards the seed He has sown in our souls. He is present in the darkest, coldest night of midwinter, even though at times He seems to have removed Himself utterly. But He is ever present. Like the leek, we are growing under His hand. It is in the winter of nature that we harvest our leeks and at the end of Advent that we have sight of His glory: 'You also be patient. Establish your hearts, for the coming of the Lord is at hand' (*Jm* 5:8).

The **Potato**, that noble and solid staple, has the traditional meaning of benevolence. It can therefore be associated with many saints, particularly those who gave away their own earthly riches to work among the poor. It always reminds me of Saint Louise de Marillac (1591-1660) who co-founded the Daughters of Charity with Saint Vincent de Paul. As her spiritual director he had counselled her and her first companions: 'Your convent will be the house of the sick, your cell a rented room, your chapel the parish church, your cloister the city streets and hospital corridors, your enclosure obedience, your grille fear of God, your veil modesty.' On or around Saint Louise's day (March 15), when I buy my seed potatoes, I remember all the Vincentians I have known, and with special gratitude and love, Sister Agnes, the white Daughter of Charity, who brought me into the Church. As I set the seed to 'chit' I commit to Jesus, all city dwellers, particularly those who reject or do not know Him; every time I inspect the length of the sprouts from the 'eyes' I ask the Holy Spirit for grace, that I may grow in humility and love. Digging the trenches, I offer all my gardening and domestic work to Christ. Setting the seed in the earth, my prayer to the Holy Trinity asks for strength, truth and creativity in my teaching and writing and concludes in thanksgiving for grace already bestowed. At each 'earthing up' I ask for God's continued protection of Our Holy Father and of us all, and at crop lifting, I beg to be able to go at last to meet Our Lord, bearing fruits acceptable to Him.

Weeds and poisonous plants as a stimulus to meditation

Nor do I disdain **Weeds**, or even poisonous plants, as a stimulus to meditation. In the past **Shepherd's Needle** has led me to a reflection on neighbourliness; **Speedwell** to one on faithfulness and **Blessed Thistle** to thoughts on the holiness attained by the young Aloysius Gonzaga. (Many plants, because of their symbolism and alternative names can represent several people or things. When visiting the '*Carduus Benedictus*', the Blessed or Holy Thistle I may pray for our Holy Father and his intentions or reflect on an aspect of his teaching; I could study a page of St Benedict's Rule; or simply pray for all Benedictines).

Dock, with its deep rooted tenacity and terrible self-seeding propensities, led to a consideration of the nature of sin, while **Corncockle**, detested by farmers, was offered to Saint James the Greater as a 'lily of the field', mainly because Santiago di Compostella means 'St James of the Field of Stars'. And yet Dock has the famous property of soothing nettle stings, although I have to speak up in preference for **Lemon Balm** here, (also known as 'Sweet Mary') and **Corncockle** is beautiful if kept away from fields of grain.

Most weeds do in fact have redeeming features: it is just that they insist on growing where they are not wanted. At least in that, they share a characteristic with sin itself.

Shakespeare, in the guise of Friar Lawrence reflects:

'Within the infant rind of this weak flower
Poison hath residence, and medicine power,
Two such opposed kings encamp them still,
In man as well as herbs – grace and rude will:
And where the worser is predominant,
Full soon the canker death eats up the plant.'

And so, whether a plant leads me to meditation and prayer or whether I have to look for a plant to suit a particular liturgical theme or saint's day, the amazing fact is that so far the right one has always suggested itself in one way or another. And yet, I should not really be surprised, because the instinct of faith told me beforehand that it must be so.

Note on houseplants

Dr Hessayon's *'The Gold Plated House plant Expert'* is indispensable.[8] A holy indoor conservatory can be made of many plants that have Christian connotations, for example **Rosary Vine**, **Crown of Thorns**, **Peace Lily**, **Bird of Paradise**, and **Angel's Wing Begonis**.

An epilogue of roses

One could plant an entire garden of roses whose names or history have Christian significance.[9] Several have already been mentioned in these pages. Here are some more from my garden. All except 'Ash Wednesday' are fragrant, those marked *ef* exceptionally so.

Breath of Life – Soft apricot climber (For the Pro-life movement.

Ash Wednesday – Dull white climber.

Fellowship – Orange to scarlet floribunda.

The Pilgrim – *ef* pale yellow English rose.

Heritage – *ef* medium pink (for the 40 Martyrs of England and Wales).

Pride of England – Medium red Hybrid Tea (For SS John Fisher and Thomas More).

St Dunstan's Rose – *ef* white or yellow Shrub Rose.

Felicity Perpetue – cream climber.

Blessings – coral peach hybrid tea.

The Compassionate Friends – *ef* medium pink floribunda.

Danse du Feu – orange to scarlet climber (Pentecost).

Dame du Coeur – dark red hybrid tea (Immaculate Heart of Mary).

And for the future

St Pier – Medium pink shrub (for our present Holy Father).
The Doctor – Medium Pink hybrid tea (Doctors of the Church, particularly for Hildegard of Bingen).

Envoi

As the Easter Lily blooms, may you meet the risen Lord and hasten into the world with the Good News; when the swallow is on the wing, may you rejoice in the Spirit and receive His gifts; at the season of sowing and planting may you grow in the Word; and at the time of reaping, may you joyfully bear a rich harvest home to God. Amen.

Endnotes

[1] In 1981 Pope Benedict, then Archbishop of Munich, wrote a series of five superb catechetical homilies on the Creation accounts in Genesis. These were republished in English as *In the Beginning... A Catholic Understanding of Creation and the Fall* (Continuum 1995).

[2] For detailed information see: *www.newadvent.org/cathen/12149a.htm Plants, Flowers and Herbs of the Bible* – W. E. Shewell-Cooper 1988 Keats Publishing Connecticut. (An indispensable volume usually available at amazon.com, although not to my knowledge at amazon.co.uk).

[3] *www.edenproject.com.*

[4] For quiet gardens to visit, contact The Quiet Garden Trust or go to them at *www.quietgarden.org.*

[5] See *www.OrganicCatalogue.com* for all organic gardening needs including wild flower and vegetable seeds and reasonably priced organic instruction leaflets for composting, weed and pest control etc. Browse and order on line or send for a copy from The Organic Catalogue, Riverdene, Molesey Road, Hersham, Surrey KT12 4RG.

[6] The language of flowers Wikipedia page gives comprehensive list and several other useful links.

[7] The meditation can be found on my blog at: *thoughtsfromoasisinfrenchcatholicism.blogspot.com* in the blog archive at December 7th and 8th 2008.

[8] I'm not sure it is still in print but at present writing copies are available at Amazon.co.uk. (hardback over 250 pages with photographs).

[9] *Find that Rose.* See *www.findthatrose.net* annually published catalogue of includes full description of all roses available in Britain, with suppliers' addresses - Write to: The Editor, 303 Mile End Road, Colchester, CO4 5EA.

Litany of Loreto

This litany to the Blessed Virgin Mary was first used in the mid-16th century at the Italian shrine from which its name derives. Now considered a classic text of Marian devotion, the Litany of Loreto is an opportunity to draw closer to Jesus' mother through seeing her as the greatest example of the Christian life.

This booklet, as well as containing the full text of the actual litany, also looks closely at the many titles used to describe Our Blessed Lady and how their meaning can help us to live as she did, ever open to God's plan.

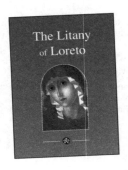

ISBN: 978 1 86082 796 9

CTS Code: D 751

Conversational Prayer

A constant friendship with Jesus

Conversational prayer brings us closer to Jesus: it's a friendship form of prayer - it can be done while 'on the go', that is, while working, travelling, shopping, and so forth.

Throughout this booklet conversational prayer is written about as a conversation with Jesus - and also with our Father, with the Holy Spirit, with Our Lady, Saint Joseph, the other Saints and your Guardian Angel.

Perhaps you too will start, if you haven't already, to engage in conversational prayer. It is not a matter of abandoning other forms of prayer, just of praying more.

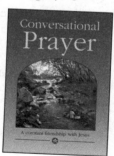

ISBN: 978 1 86082 665 8
CTS Code: D 728